S0-FCZ-822

SEQUOYAH REGIONAL LIBRARY

3 8749 0019 6455 8

GREAT GUARDS

Marty Nabhan

BASKETBALL HEROES

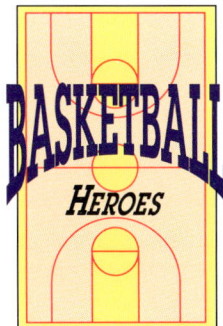

The Rourke Corporation, Inc.
Vero Beach, Florida 32964

THIS BOOK IS THE PROPERTY OF
SEQUOYAH REGIONAL LIBRARY
CANTON, GEORGIA

Copyright 1992 by The Rourke Corporation, Inc.

All rights reserved. No part of this book may be reproduced or utilized in any form or by any means, electronic or mechanical, including photocopying, recording or by any information storage and retrieval system without permission in writing from the publisher.

The Rourke Corporation, Inc.
P.O. Box 3328, Vero Beach, FL 32964

Nabhan, Marty.
    Great guards / by Marty Nabhan.
        p. cm. — (Basketball heroes)
    Includes bibliographical references (p.47) and index.
    Summary: Discusses the role of guards in professional basketball and describes the play of some of the game's best, including Michael Jordan, Jerry West, and Magic Johnson.
    ISBN 0-86593-159-3
    1. Basketball — Offense — Juvenile literature. 2. Guards (Basketball) — United States — Biography — Juvenile literature. [1. Guards (Basketball) 2. Basketball.] I. Title. II. Series.
GV889.N33   1992
769.323'2 —dc20   92-8761
                                                                                  CIP
                                                                                   AC

Series Editor: Gregory Lee
Editor: Marguerite Aronowitz
Book design and production: The Creative Spark, San Clemente, CA
Cover photograph: Tim DeFrisco/ALLSPORT USA

Contents

The tongue is out, which means, "Look out! Here comes Mr. Jordan!"

Michael Jordan: Up, Up And Away

Jordan wept. Michael Jordan, a guard for the Chicago Bulls, held the championship trophy in his hands. He leaned his head on it and closed his eyes. Tears flowed. But they were not tears of sadness or sorrow. They were tears of joy, tears of gratitude, tears of relief, tears of love.

Michael Jordan is different than most players in the National Basketball Association (NBA). He's special. Of the 300-plus players in the league, he has often been called the best. Some people have called him the greatest to ever play the game. But he had never won an NBA championship.

That's not to say that his life had been without honors. After a college championship, Jordan led the United States' basketball team to a gold medal in the 1984 Olympics. In that same year, he was the third player taken in the basketball draft, and the first pick of the Chicago Bulls.

The Chicago Bulls were not a very good team in 1984. They had not reached the playoffs in years. So the Bulls put the ball in Jordan's hands, hoping he could turn things around.

So Jordan shot. And scored. And scored some

more. But it wasn't just Jordan's scoring that made him a great guard. It was the *way* he did it. Every time he touched the ball, Jordan created a new move. Leaping from the free-throw line for a slam dunk? No problem. Switching hands in mid-shot? Easy. Twisting around defenders to shoot an off-balance shot? Nothing to it.

Jordan made it all look as natural as, well, flying. At times he seemed to float in mid-air. First he would approach the basket with his tongue hanging out. Then he would take another step and—blast off! He was airborne. Fans said Jordan spent more time above the court than on it. They even started calling him "Air Jordan."

Jordan was unstoppable. Other teams tried to keep the ball from him, but he always seemed to be in the right place at the right time. He led the NBA in scoring for five seasons in a row (from 1987 to 1991). No other player had done that since Wilt Chamberlain in the 1960s. It was not surprising to see Jordan score 40 or 50 points in one game.

But was it enough to be one of the game's greatest scorers ever? No. Jordan wanted to show he could do more. In 1988 he worked on his defense and was named "Defensive Player of the Year." He also won the award for Most Valuable Player that year, an award he won again in 1991.

In Jordan's first season the Bulls made the playoffs. It was their first time in four years. In 1987 the Bulls won 40 games, ten more than the year before. It was also the first year Jordan led the league in scoring. In the next three years the Bulls won 50, 47, and 55 games.

But there were critics of Jordan's style. Some people said the team with the best scorer couldn't win the championship. Maybe they were right. Every year, rival teams would focus on Jordan in the playoffs. And

Isiah Thomas and the Detroit Pistons were not firing on all cylinders when the Bulls took them out of the 1991 playoffs in four straight games.

every year the Bulls came up short. No team with the league's best scorer had won the finals in 20 years. The last team to do that was the Milwaukee Bucks, with Kareem Abdul-Jabbar, in 1971.

In 1991 the Bulls had the best record in basketball: 61 wins and only 21 losses. Jordan again led the league in scoring with 31.5 points per game. But he also passed the ball more. He involved his teammates. With Jordan leading the way, the rest of his teammates improved. Scottie Pippen became a true star. John Paxson shot well. Horace Grant got more rebounds.

The 1991 playoffs began. First the Bulls knocked off the New York Knicks in four straight games. Then

Michael Jordan led the Chicago Bulls to the NBA finals in 1991
with his league-leading scoring and strong defense.

they brushed past the Philadelphia 76ers.

The Eastern finals pitted the Bulls against the Detroit Pistons. The Pistons had knocked the Bulls out of the playoffs for the last three years. But 1991 was a different story. The Bulls swept the Pistons in four games.

Just one thing stood between Michael Jordan and the championship trophy: Magic Johnson and the Los Angeles Lakers. In Game 1, with just 14 seconds left to play, Laker Sam Perkins made a three-point shot. But the Bulls still had a chance to win the game. With nine seconds left, Jordan missed a short shot. The Lakers won in Chicago, 92-91.

In Game 2, the Bulls played a near-perfect game.

Jordan and his teammates built up a big lead over the Lakers. Then, in the fourth quarter, Jordan made "The Shot." He leapt into the air. He wanted to slam dunk with his right hand, but too many Lakers were there. Still in mid-air, he shifted the ball into his left hand. Then just before he touched the floor, he flipped the ball in with his left. The shot was a classic—the stuff of highlight films—and Jordan never looked back. Final score: Bulls 107, Lakers 86.

In the next three games, the Lakers tried to double- and triple-team Jordan. He simply threw the ball to another player for an easy shot. In Game 3, the Bulls trailed 92-90. With a few seconds left, Jordan sunk a 14-foot shot to tie. The Bulls won in overtime. Game 4 was never close, as Jordan's Bulls beat the Lakers 97-82. The Bulls wrapped it up in Game 5, 108-101.

Jordan had wanted a championship more than anything, and now he had it. After the game the team huddled in the locker room for a prayer. Then they celebrated. Jordan held the championship trophy. It had taken seven years in the NBA for him to win it. He had proved the critics wrong.

"In the pros, I've seen the struggles," Jordan said. "All the people saying, 'He's not going to win.' You have doubts. But you have to put them aside and think positive."

He was asked about the championship ring.. "I'm going to pass it on down to my kids. No one can take it away from me. I don't know if I'll ever have this feeling again. All the things I've gone through. It was a lot of hard work. What you see is the emotions of all that hard work paying off."

So Jordan wept. He had worked for an NBA championship, and now it was done. He had sailed from the court into the sky and was called the greatest ever. He may never touch down again.

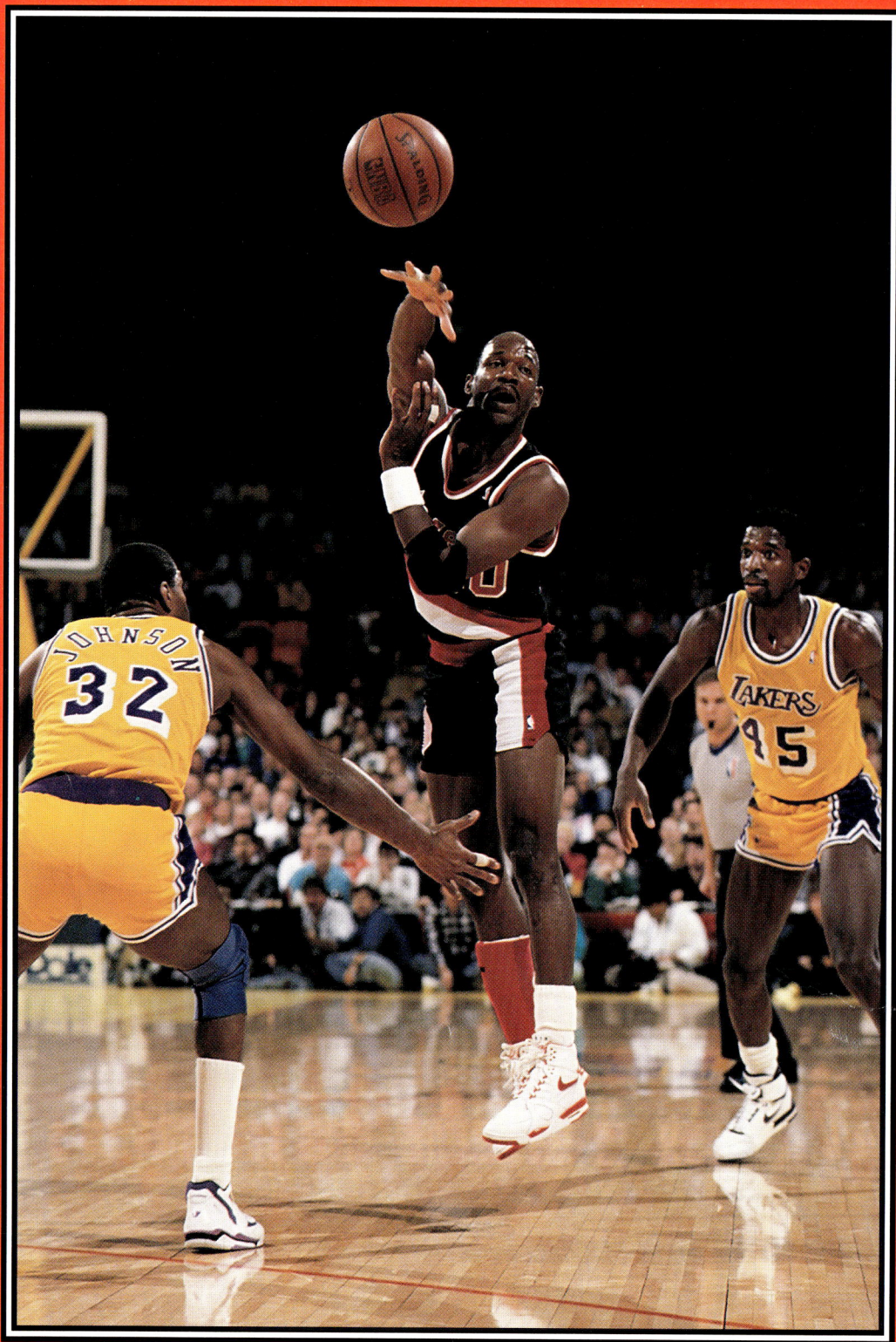

Key passing is a must for a great guard—something Terry Porter loves to do.

Changing Of The Guard

Players in all positions learn the basics. They know how to dribble, pass, and shoot. They must be in good shape to be able to run up and down the court. They should all have a sense of what it takes to help their team win.

But guards must also have certain special skills. They are assigned to a specific area of the court. This area is called the *perimeter,* the area of the court between the half-court line and the three-point line.

Guards cover a lot of territory. Therefore, they have to be quick. They are usually skilled at bouncing or dribbling the ball. Guards also need to be good passers to get the ball to other teammates inside the perimeter.

Guards play farther away from the basket than the other players. They need the ability to shoot well

Guard Trivia

Q: Name the guard who has won more NBA Most Valuable Player awards in championship play than anyone else.

A: Earvin "Magic" Johnson of the Los Angeles Lakers, with three (1980, 1982, 1987).

Q: Only one player in the history of basketball won the Most Valuable Player award in the championship series while playing for the losing team. Who was this guard?

A: Jerry West of the Los Angeles Lakers, 1969.

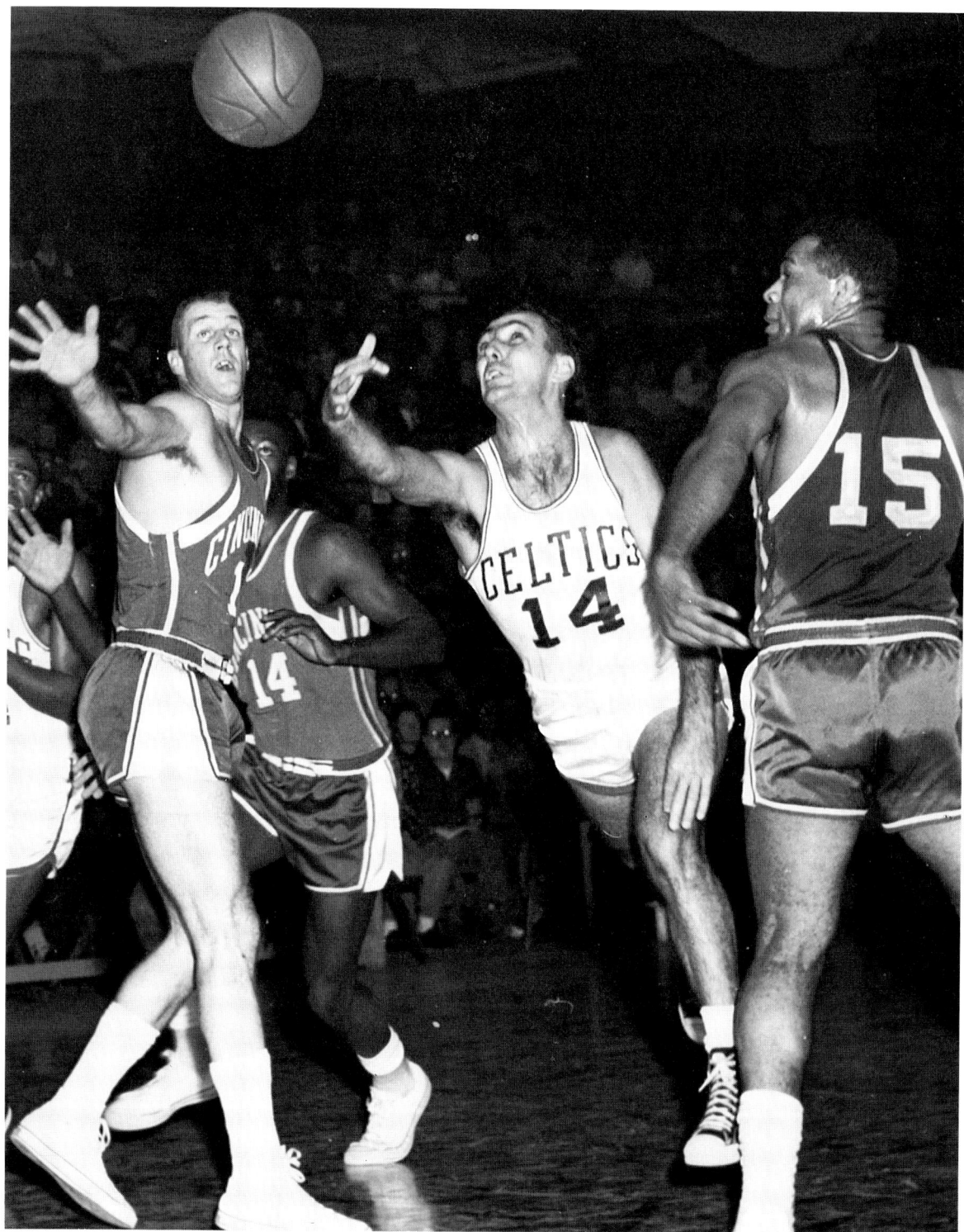

Bob Cousy was the first great guard of the modern NBA era.
His electric work with the Boston Celtics won many
championships.

from the outside. When a shooter misses a shot, the players near the basket jump for the rebound. Since guards do not play close to the basket, they do not have to rebound as often. Therefore, they do not need to be the tallest players. Guards are often the shortest players on the team.

Guards come in all shapes and sizes. And as the game of basketball has changed over the years, guards have changed with it.

The Early Days

Basketball was invented 100 years ago by Dr. James Naismith. Naismith was a physical education teacher for the YMCA in Springfield, Massachusetts. Winters are cold in Massachusetts. Naismith's class had to exercise indoors because of the weather. Naismith wanted to create a sport that his students could play indoors during the winter, so he nailed peach baskets to the balcony railing of the gym, 10 feet off the floor.

Naismith's class had 18 students. Therefore, the first basketball games had nine players on each team. The games were rough and wild, and the players loved them.

After each basket, the game was stopped. A man with a ladder walked onto the court. He set the ladder by the basket, climbed up, and took out the ball. The game was then ready to start again. Finally, to speed up the game, the bottoms were taken out of the peach baskets.

The first great guard of this faster game was Barney Sedran. Sedran was only five-feet, four-inches tall, but he led his team to 35 victories in a row. There were no backboards behind the basket in those days, but that didn't keep Sedran from scoring a lot of points.

New rules helped speed up the game. In 1937 they did away with the *jump ball* after every basket. Teams could immediately run up the court after a score. In 1954 the game was made even faster by the use of a "24-second clock." Teams had 24 seconds to shoot after they got the ball. If they did not shoot by then, the other team got the ball back.

These two rules really helped shape professional basketball. And the guard who made the most of his skills in this faster game was Bob Cousy. Cousy played for the Boston Celtics. He led the Celtics to many championships during his career. Only six-feet, one-inch, Cousy had a great ability to see all of the court while looking straight ahead. This good vision helped him pass the ball well and fake out opponents. The Celtics could always count on Cousy to get the ball into the right player's hands.

Cousy ran Boston's *fast break*. A fast break is an attempt to beat the other team to the basket they are defending. Often Cousy would outrun the other team. He would then take the easy shot. If there were defenders in the way, Cousy would pass the ball and his teammate would score. Passing to a teammate who scores is called an *assist*.

Sometimes Cousy passed behind his back. He invented that move. His amazing passes, his quickness, his knowledge of where his teammates were at all times—these things made Cousy great.

Cousy retired in 1963, but his style of play remained popular. In the 1960s and 1970s, teams continued to run fast breaks. There were always new players, but the game stayed pretty much the same.

It stayed the same, that is, until 1980.

Today's Guard

In the 1960s and 1970s, centers won basketball games. They were the tallest players. They were the highest scorers. They led the defense.

Magic Johnson broke the mold of the small guard forever.

In 1980 the Los Angeles Lakers had one of the best centers: Kareem Abdul-Jabbar. At the end of the season, they were playing for the NBA championship. Although they led the Philadelphia 76ers three games to two, things suddenly took a bad turn. At the end of Game 5, Kareem injured his ankle. Most people expected the Lakers to lose Game 6 without him. But not Earvin "Magic" Johnson. He expected to win.

Johnson was the Lakers' rookie guard. But when he stepped on the court for Game 6, it was in Kareem's center position! The other players were shocked at the coach's decision. A guard playing a position reserved for the tallest man on the court? It was unheard of.

"It was all I could do to keep from laughing," Johnson said. It may have seemed like a joke to the

"Spud" Webb proves that there's life for short guards—even those who are under six-feet tall.

76ers, but by game's end they weren't laughing. Magic had played all five positions in one of the greatest performances in NBA Finals history. He finished with 42 points, 15 rebounds, seven assists, five steals and a blocked shot. The Lakers won the game and the series, and Magic was named the series' Most Valuable Player. It was the beginning of a revolution in the NBA.

Suddenly, teams wanted great guards. Not just guards who could shoot. They wanted guards who could rebound, guards who could find the open man, guards who could defend. They wanted guards who could control a game.

Because of Magic Johnson's success, teams wanted taller guards. Players who were forwards in college learned to play guard. Sidney Moncrief, Kendall Gill, Michael Jordan, and Clyde Drexler all fit the mold of "big guards."

Many guards are still the smallest players. In the 1970s, six-foot, one-inch guard Nate Archibald was considered small. His nickname was "Tiny." Today, most teams have guards under six-feet, one-inch. Anthony "Spud" Webb once won the All-Star slam dunk contest. Webb is five-feet, seven-inches. Tyrone "Muggsy" Bogues led the Charlotte Hornets in assists and steals. Bogues is five-feet, three-inches! He showed that size is not an obstacle.

Today's guards each have their specialties. Some are very quick. Some are great shooters. Some have a great sense of teamwork and like to pass the ball. In today's NBA there are two types of guards: point guards and shooting guards.

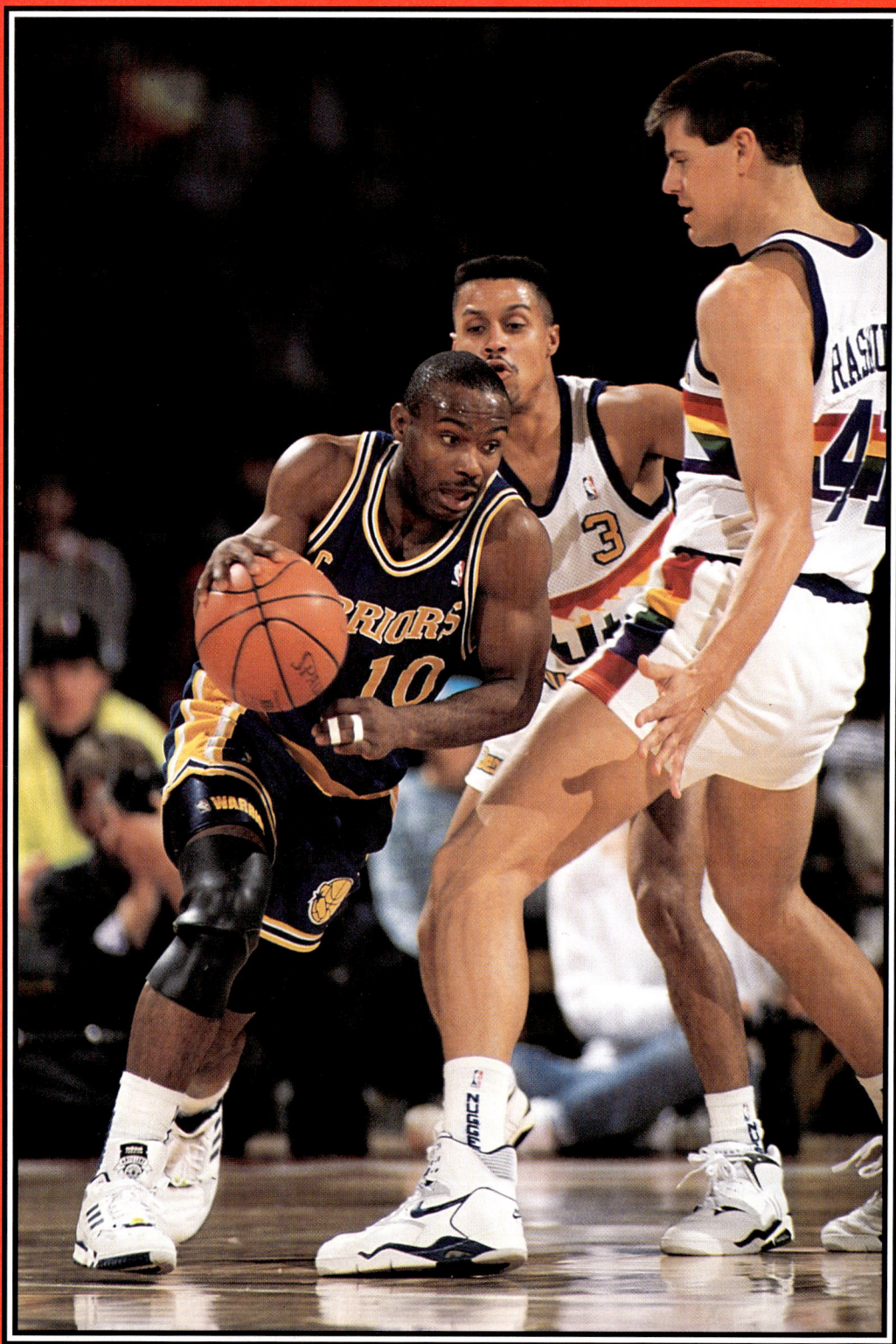

Tim Hardaway's dribbling, passing, and shooting skills made him an All-Star pick in just his second pro year.

The Modern Basketball Quarterback

The point guard dribbles up the court. A player from the other team runs in front of him, trying to steal the ball. The point guard dribbles behind his back and steps easily around the defender. He comes into the front court. He continues to dribble. All the while, he watches his teammates. *Which one of them has the best shot at the basket?* he wonders. Suddenly, a teammate spins away from a defender under the basket. The point guard sees this out of the corner of his eye. With lightning-quick hands he snaps the ball up toward the basket.

A focused Mark Price drives around the defense.

His open teammate leaps into the air. He catches the ball above the rim of the basket and stuffs it through.

A play like the *alley-oop* takes timing, practice, and skill. Those are just three of the talents of the point guard. A point guard has the ability to see and react quickly to situations. He sets the pace of the offense. His most important duties are ball handling and assisting teammates in scoring.

Point guard is a lot like playing quarterback for a football team. In football, the quarterback gets the ball and looks over the playing field. He sees where players are and where they are going. If he sees someone in the open, he tries to pass the ball to them. That way, the player in the open might score.

A point guard does the same thing. He looks over the court. He dribbles while his teammates keep moving. He finds an open man and passes the ball. If that man shoots and scores, the point guard gets an assist.

Ballhandling

It is fun to watch a skilled player handle the ball. In the 1970s, Atlanta Hawks and New Orleans Jazz star "Pistol" Pete Maravich excited crowds with fancy passes between his legs and behind his back. Earl "The Pearl" Monroe of the Baltimore Bullets and the New York Knicks amazed fans with his spinning moves to the basket.

Dribbling the ball under pressure is an important skill, and point guards handle the ball more than any other player. Sometimes teams try to take the ball away from the point guard as he makes his way down the court. This is called a *full court press*. But it's hard to steal the ball from a fast point guard.

One of the best ball handlers in the league is Tim Hardaway. Hardaway is very quick. He switches hands with his dribble faster than a defender can react. Back and forth he goes, right hand to left hand. When the

One of the hardest working guards in the business—on offense or defense—is Kevin Johnson.

defender leans one way, Hardaway goes the other. Other defenders may try to help, but Hardaway often spots his open teammate for the quick score.

"Even in his rookie season, I thought his crossover move was one of the most wicked I'd ever seen," opponent Magic Johnson once said. "But he's perfected it. It's beautiful to watch. It's amazing."

Hardaway can shoot well, too. "He's like Mighty Mouse," said Golden State coach Don Nelson. "When things look tough, he saves the day." Hardaway was chosen to play in the All-Star game in just his second year. Hardaway is young, and will be an All-Star for years to come.

Kevin Johnson is another great young point guard.

Johnson is a very quick player with a great fast break. He has the ability to sprint up the court and score quickly, driving to the basket and cutting through defenses. Kevin Johnson is also a good outside shooter. "KJ" is only the second player in NBA history to average more than 20 points and 10 assists for three seasons in a row.

Johnson strives for excellence on and off the court. In 1991 he received the Citizenship Award, given to the player who does great things for his community. KJ does charity work for the kids in the neighborhood where he grew up. He started the St. Hope Academy to help children from the ghetto. He also received one of President Bush's Point of Light awards.

Michael Adams is a point guard with scoring on his mind. At five-feet, eleven-inches, Adams has been called a "tiny tornado" as he runs down the court. He moves from side to side, spinning as he goes. His swift passes placed him third in assists in 1991. His scoring was also high, averaging 26.5 points per game. Because his teams have rarely made the playoffs, Adams might be the best kept secret in the NBA.

Adams once tied the NBA record for most three-pointers in one game (9). He is also the league's all-time leader in career three-pointers.

Assists

Getting assists shows that a guard cares about winning, because a good point guard needs to be a great team player. Good eyesight is also a plus. Some people think a point guard has eyes in the back of his head. Watching some blind passes, it's not hard to believe.

Oscar Robertson of the Milwaukee Bucks was one of the all-time great passers. His scoring and rebound abilities were also incredible. But "The Big O" was known mainly for his 9,887 career assists, a record that stood until Magic Johnson broke it in 1991.

Until the Magic Johnson era, no one had more assists than Oscar Robertson, with 9,887. His jump shot looked pretty good, too.

Experts say that John Stockton is the best passer in basketball today. It would be hard to argue with them. Stockton is quick. He knows where his teammates are at all times, and he finds the open man. They get the points; he gets the assists.

In fact, Stockton has led the league in assists for four years in a row, passing for more than 1,000 assists each year. No other player has ever had 1,000 assists per season more than once. In 1991, Stockton set a record with 1,164. Whose record did he break? His own, set the year before.

The assists master of the decade is John Stockton of the Utah Jazz.

Stockton has been compared to Bob Cousy. Stockton is short like Cousy, and he can make amazing passes, especially to teammate Karl Malone.

Scott Skiles is another fireball. "I don't know what or how it happens," Skiles said. "When I compete, I kind of act like that guy who turns into a werewolf when the moon is full."

Skiles churns around the court like a runaway train. He dives for loose balls. He yells at the other team. He shoots from a distance. And he holds an NBA record: most assists in a single game. On December 30, 1990, Skiles gave out 30 assists against the Denver Nuggets. That year he placed tenth in assists, sixth in free throws, and fifth in three-point shots. He was also named the NBA's Most Improved Player.

"There's one thing I hate worse than losing and that's people who don't play hard all the time," Skiles said. "So with me you always get the effort."

Top Competitors

Point guards help their teams win. When they play well, they help their teammates play well. Terry Porter is one such player. He doesn't have flashy statistics, but he is always reliable. He is one of the big reasons the Portland Trailblazers have risen to the top of the Western Conference in recent years.

Porter's job is to make sure his team wins. He does everything well. He is also one of the best three-point shooters in the NBA, hitting 42 percent of his shots.

"A lot of the point guards are so much the focal point of their team," Porter said. "It's not important for me to score twenty points or have the ball ninety percent of the time."

On the other hand, when the game is on the line, Isiah Thomas wants the ball. He rarely misses a shot in the last few minutes of a game. He is an intense player,

At just 6'1", Isiah Thomas may not seem imposing, but his play has led the Detroit Pistons to back-to-back NBA championships.

and is a natural playmaker. Thomas makes good decisions on the court, often grinning while he's at work.

But don't let Thomas fool you. Behind that impish grin is a hard-working competitor. He loves to compete, but he loves to win even more. He sparked the Detroit Pistons to two championships in 1989 and 1990.

"When I was a little kid," Thomas said, "I never let size become an issue. The main thing is developing your skills and using the talent that God has given you. Good players come in all different packages."

An injury to his wrist has recently slowed Thomas down. But he will still be ranked as one of the best guards in the modern NBA era.

Derek Harper has grown in value to the Dallas Mavericks. He is the first player ever to have improved his scoring every year since he's been in the league (he was a rookie in 1983). Harper is especially good at leading his team on fast breaks. He is one of the best at making the perfect pass.

Two other young point guards have been burning up the court lately. Dee Brown shows some of the best speed in basketball. And Brian Shaw led the Boston Celtics in assists in 1990. They will be helping their teammates win for a long time to come.

Johnny Dawkins is another top player. He is obviously valuable to his team, because when he is injured his team does not play as well.

Finally, Mark Price has been called the best point guard in the East. He certainly means a lot to his team. The Cleveland Cavaliers expected a big season in 1990-91, but when Price was injured, so was the Cavs' season. It is hard for a team to play without its quarterback.

Bob Cousy once summed up the role of the point guard: "If the guy comes across half court and thinks about passing first and shooting second, then he's a real point guard."

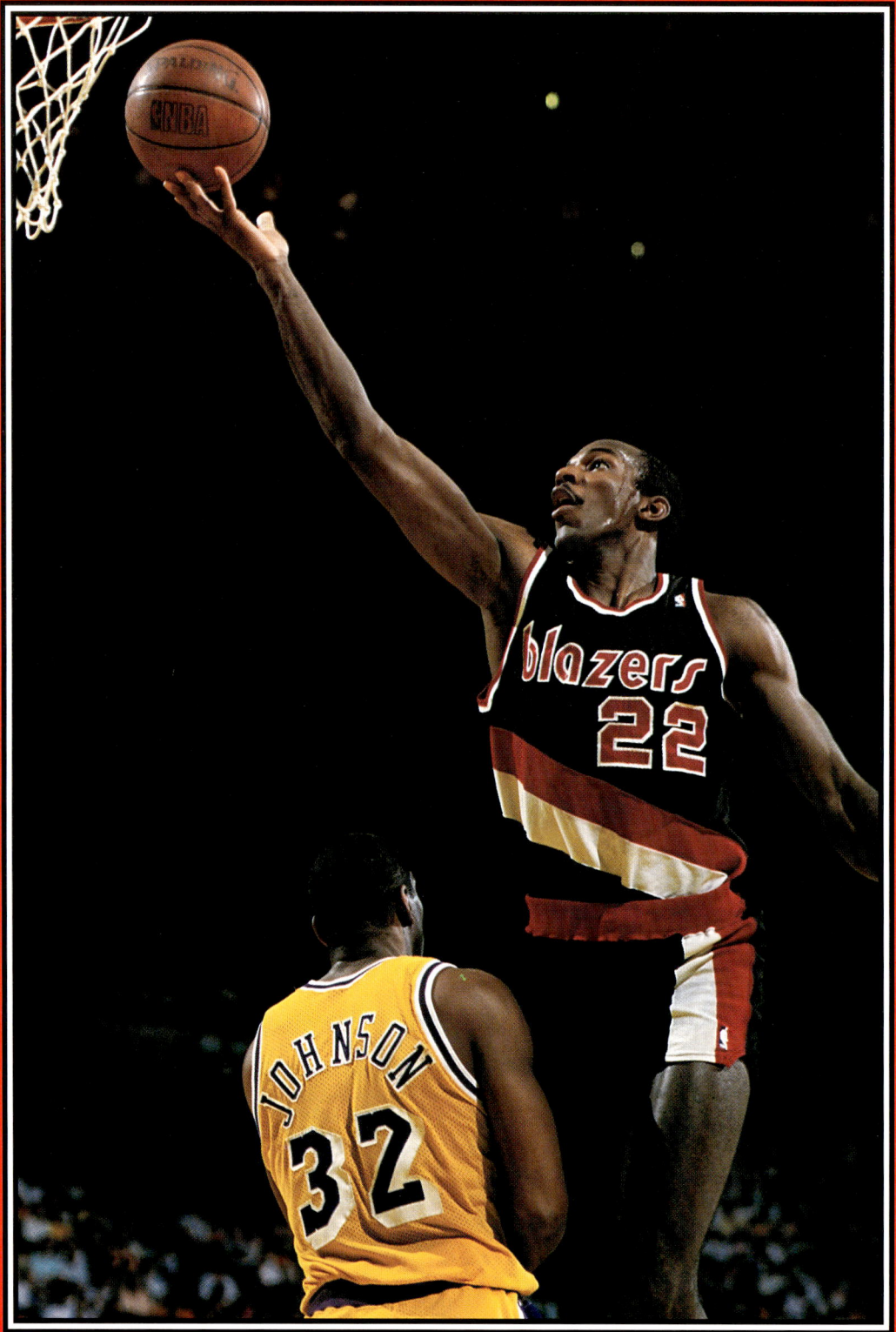

Fans don't call him Clyde "the Glide" Drexler for nothing.

Shooting Stars And Defense

The shooting guard looks at the 24-second clock. There are eight seconds left. The point guard has the ball at the top of the key. The shooting guard knows it is time to get open, but his defender is guarding closely. The shooting guard runs toward the basket. The defender tries to cut him off. The shooting guard turns and runs by his own teammate. His teammate executes a *screen*, standing in the way of the defender. Now the open shooting guard receives the pass and jumps, squaring his shoulders to the basket. At the top of his jump, he releases the ball. As the seconds tick off, he sees the ball glide through the hoop with a swoosh.

Shooting is the most visible part of the game. Everyone can see a player shoot. Everyone knows if the shot is good. But there

Guard Trivia

Q: In 1991, John Stockton won his fourth consecutive assist title. Who holds the record for most consecutive seasons leading the league in assists?

A: Bob Cousy of the Boston Celtics with eight, from 1953-1960.

Q: From 1958 through 1986, the winners of the Podoloff Trophy for Most Valuable Player during the regular season were all either centers or forwards. Who was the guard to break this string in 1987?

A: Magic Johnson of the Los Angeles Lakers.

is more to being a shooting guard than good aim. The best shooting guards know how to get open. They know how to shake a defender. They know where to move without the ball. They also know when to shoot and when to pass instead.

The Development of Shooting

The early basketball shooters had a hard job. Not only did they have to shoot over the hands of defenders, but fans would often knock the ball away from the basket! Fans sitting behind the railing that held the basket would stick their foot in the way of a shot. Others even used umbrellas to block the shot. The first backboards were invented, therefore, to keep fans from interfering with the game.

Backboards also improved shooting. They gave players something to aim at. Some shooters used the backboards to bounce their shots into the basket. Those shots are still called *bank shots*.

The most popular shot in early basketball was the *set shot*. The shooter kept both feet on the floor. He held the ball with both hands. From his chest, he threw the ball at the basket. This two-handed set shot was used in basketball for many years.

As a young boy in the 1930s, Angelo "Hank" Luisetti was not coordinated enough to shoot with two hands. Instead, he threw the ball at the basket with one hand. Other players tried the one-handed shot. Today no one uses the old, two-hand set shot.

One of the legendary shooters of all time was Jerry West of the Los Angeles Lakers. In the 1960s and 1970s, West was famous for making shots in the last few seconds of a game. His nickname was "Mr. Clutch." In 1969 West was named MVP of the championship series, even though his Lakers lost to the Boston Celtics.

In 1970 West made what might be the most

Jerry West of the Los Angeles Lakers was "Mr. Clutch," because he always scored when the game was on the line. Here he dribbles past the defense of Walt Frazier, the Knicks' Hall of Fame forward.

famous shot in the history of basketball. The Lakers were playing the New York Knicks for the championship. The Knicks had scored to go ahead 102-100. With three seconds left, West got the ball near his basket. Taking two steps, he fired. The ball sailed through the air 63 feet and went straight into the Knicks' basket. Unfortunately, the shot only tied the game, and the Lakers lost in overtime. In those days, there was no such thing as a three-point shot to save the game.

A dependable passer and shooter for ten years—
that's Rolando Blackman.

The *three-point shot* is a long distance shot. A line on the court marks the distance. Since it is harder to shoot that far, the shot is worth three points.

The three-point shot was used in the American Basketball Association (ABA) for many years. In 1979 it was introduced to the NBA. At first teams did not use it much. Players usually went for it in the final minutes as a last chance to win. In today's game, however, many players are good at the three-point shot.

Offensive Weapons

Shooting guards in the NBA today are better than ever. Perhaps the best of them is Michael Jordan. If there is a type of shot Jordan hasn't made, it hasn't been invented. His drive, scoring, and teamwork led to a Bulls championship in 1991.

Teammate John Paxson has said, "Michael is the greatest athlete in the sport, maybe in the world."

"He's almost super-human," said Laker coach Mike Dunleavy. "I don't know if anything works on him. He's capable of winning games by himself."

Shooting guard Clyde Drexler also helps his team win. At six-feet, seven-inches, "Clyde the Glide" is an all-around player. He scores. He rebounds. He runs hard on every play. Drexler has been compared to Michael Jordan in his ability to make great plays. He is the best shooting guard in the West.

"He's one of the best athletes to ever play in the NBA," said one scout. "He has the quickest first three steps I've ever seen. If there's a loose ball, he's going to get it."

One of the newest shooting stars is Reggie Miller. Miller is one of the best long-range shooters in the game. He's good at driving to the basket, and he can make a basket from almost anywhere. In 1991, only four players made more three-pointers than Miller did while he played

Hustle is that extra effort put into every minute a player is on the floor.

for the Indiana Pacers. He also led the league that year in free throw shooting, hitting almost 92 percent.

"I play for my teammates and the adults, but I really play for the kids," Miller said. "I play to see a kid's reaction—'Oh, man, did you see that?'—that's what I really love."

When the opponent is tough, Miller gets better. In the playoffs he scored whenever he wanted to. "I love going against Michael Jordan," Miller said. "I get up for everyone, but I especially get up for him."

Jeff Hornacek, the six-feet, four-inch shooting guard rarely makes a mistake. "He's the best shooter on our team," said Phoenix Suns coach Cotton Fitzsimmons. "He's also the kind of smart player you want in there making decisions when the game is on the line."

Hornacek always seems to do the right thing to spark his team. He knows when to take the three-point shot. He makes the shot 42 percent of the time, third best in the NBA.

Joe Dumars is quiet and soft-spoken, but on the court his actions speak loudly. Dumars won the Most Valuable Player award in the 1989 NBA Finals playing for the Detroit Pistons. He can shoot under pressure, and his defense is tough. When teammate Isiah Thomas was injured, Dumars took up the slack. He improved in scoring and assists. He led his team in scoring, field goals, free throws, and steals.

Dumars is tough. In 1991 he had an injured toe all year. It hurt so much that he had to cut a hole in his shoe to give it room. He played much of the year like that, but never complained.

Mitch Richmond earned fame at Golden State where the six-foot, five-inch shooter teamed up with Tim Hardaway and Chris Mullin to form a dangerous shooting threesome. Together they averaged more than 70 points a game, and Richmond was named Rookie of the Year in 1989.

At the beginning of the 1991-92 season, Richmond took his scoring act to Sacramento, where he continued to show he was all-star material.

Rolando Blackman has been a star shooter for the Dallas Mavericks for more than ten years. When the game is on the line, Blackman wants the ball. He is great at getting open when teammates set a screen so he can get the ball. Blackman also has a good fake. He pretends to shoot, and when the defender jumps in the air to block, Blackman dribbles around him for an easy shot.

Many other shooting guards like Hersey Hawkins, Doc Rivers, and Byron Scott add to their teams' success by shooting from the outside.

Free Throws

Good free-throw shooting is a must for a guard. The shot is only 15 feet from the basket, and no one is allowed to interfere with it. Although it is only worth one point, the free throw often decides who wins and who loses. Guards are generally the best free-throw shooters on the team. Just look at any list of great free-throw shooters and you'll see that most of them are guards.

Good form is important in shooting free throws. Most players use a one-hand set shot. But players have their own style. Some of the best in the NBA are Reggie Miller, Jeff Malone, Ricky Pierce, and Kelly Tripucka.

Defense

The two toughest teams of the 1980s were the Boston Celtics and the Los Angeles Lakers. Together they won eight of the ten championships in that decade. They often played each other for the title, and they each had a superstar.

The Celtics had forward Larry Bird. Bird was a great shooter and team player. Give Bird the ball and the team would probably score. The Lakers had Magic Johnson. It looked like magic the way the ball seemed to disappear from his hands, only to reappear in a teammate's hands for two points.

The Celtics and the Lakers both had another very important player. They were guards with special skills. They did not score the most points, and they did not get the most rebounds. Their main job was to stop the other team's superstar. They were Dennis Johnson of the Celtics and Michael Cooper of the Lakers.

Johnson and Cooper were stars on defense. Each year the NBA names the best defensive players of the year, and Johnson and Cooper were often on the list.

Dennis Johnson guarded Magic when the two teams met. He had a pressing defense. He would try to force Magic to make mistakes. Sometimes Dennis would wait for the Lakers to make a pass. Then he would step in front and steal the ball.

Michael Cooper guarded Larry Bird. He would stick to Bird like glue, using his quickness and long arms. He made it hard to pass to Bird. When the Celtics' players looked to throw the ball to Bird, they'd see Cooper all over him. Often they had to pass the ball to somebody else.

Passing, ball handling, and shooting: obvious skills that great guards have. But it doesn't do much good to score a lot of points if the other team scores more. Dennis Johnson and Michael Cooper were a big part of their teams' success. Their defense helped their teams win. It is interesting that neither the Celtics nor the Lakers have won a championship since these two players retired.

A guard needs quickness, anticipation, skill, and knowledge of the game to play good defense. The defense tries to keep the other team from scoring. This is done by keeping the ball out of the hands of high-scoring players, or guarding players closely once they have the ball.

One of the best at this type of defense is Sedale Threatt. Threatt can move quickly from side to side, making him a good defender against guards like Tim Hardaway, Kevin Johnson, and John Stockton. Threatt always seems to be in the right place at the right time. He often gets his hands on the ball. Joe Dumars is another tight defender.

Sometimes a defender will steal the ball from the offense by knocking the ball away. If a defender is quick and alert, he knows where a player will pass the ball. A defender who catches a pass meant for another player gets an *interception*. Walt Frazier, who played for the New York Knicks, was a master at stealing the ball.

Reggie Miller averages more than 22 points per game, and is an ace free-throw shooter.

Role Players

Some guards show their value in special ways. They may not start the game, but they come off the bench to give their team a lift. They are known as role players. They have a certain purpose on their team and they fill it. They concentrate on one skill and do it well.

For example, former Detroit Piston Vinnie Johnson was known as a "streak shooter." That meant he could make a lot of baskets in a row. His nickname was "The Microwave" because he could heat up quickly. He was brought into the game to score points quickly.

Danny Ainge and Jim Les have a specialty: three-point shots. They come off the bench to give their teams a long-range threat. If their teams are down by many points, these guards can hit a few three-pointers and put them right back in the game. In 1991, Les led the entire NBA in three-point shooting percentage.

The NBA has an award called "Sixth Man of the Year." It is given to the player who does not start the game, but gives crucial help as a substitute. Ricky Pierce has won the award twice with the SuperSonics. Pierce mainly helps with his effective scoring.

Dale Ellis is another scorer that helps his team. Ellis shares the record for shooting nine three-point shots in a single game.

One category cannot be measured: hustle. When a player tries as hard as he can for every minute he plays, he is hustling. He always gives the most effort. He dives for loose balls, and he plays good defense. He keeps the ball moving, and he keeps himself moving.

Sarunas Marciulionis is such a player. He is like a spark plug for his team. He plays like every moment could be his last. His extra effort and hustle are two final elements that make up a great guard.

The play and style of Earvin "Magic" Johnson has been a hit with the fans for more than a decade.

Magic Johnson: Grinnin' Time

Thursday, November 7, 1991. A crowd gathers at the Great Western Forum in Inglewood, California. For twelve years, fans have watched Magic Johnson and the Lakers play thrilling basketball here. Now the crowd is there for another reason. The people are waiting for a news conference, when Magic Johnson will have an announcement to make.

People are guessing that Magic is going to retire. Rumors are spreading quickly. Seconds tick away like the final seconds of a close game—the kind Magic would often win with a last-second shot. As Laker play-by-play announcer Chick Hearn said many times, "It's 'nervous time' at the Forum."

Time. Magic Johnson's career was a little like time standing still, because it seemed like only yesterday when Johnson entered the NBA. He had that boyish smile and a

---

Guard Trivia

Q: Who holds the NBA record for highest career scoring average in the playoffs?

A: Michael Jordan of the Chicago Bulls, with a 34.6 average.

Q: Who holds the NBA record for most points scored in a single playoff game?

A: Michael Jordan of the Chicago Bulls, with 63 points against the Boston Celtics on April 20, 1986.

childlike enthusiasm. He was Peter Pan in a Laker uniform—the boy who never grew old.

In Magic's first game as a Laker, he passed to teammate Kareem Abdul-Jabbar with three seconds left. Abdul-Jabbar made the shot to win the game. Johnson rushed over to Kareem and gave the surprised center an excited hug.

"Relax," the veteran center said. "It's just the first game. We have 81 more to go."

"You do that 81 more times," Johnson said. "We won't have any problem."

It was the beginning of "Showtime." Showtime meant fast, flashy, dazzling basketball. "Open the curtain, the show's about to begin," one might say. If Michael Jordan made every type of shot, Magic Johnson made every type of pass. Sometimes he passed without looking because he knew where his teammates were. The fans loved it.

Showtime changed the NBA. Basketball became more popular. There were more games on television. Player salaries went up. Behind it all was Johnson's grin. It was fun to watch him because he was having fun.

An important part of Showtime was "Winnin' Time." That was the name Magic gave to the time in the game when he wanted the ball. Magic won many games with time running out. Although he was known for unselfish passes and assists, Johnson often made the game-winning shots. And whenever the Lakers got to the playoffs, Johnson said that was Winnin' Time, too.

And win he did. In his 12 years in the league, the Lakers made it to the playoffs every year. Nine of those 12 years they went to the finals. Five times they won it all. Not since the Boston Celtics of the 1960s had a team dominated the game as much as the Lakers did with Magic. Friends called it "Grinnin' Time," because Johnson always flashed his famous smile.

During his career Magic was a 10-time All-Star. He led the league in assists, won the championship series MVP twice, and the league MVP three times. In 1991, he broke a record set by the legendary Oscar Robertson for most assists in a lifetime. Later that year he led the Lakers—a team many thought wouldn't make it past third place in their division—to the NBA finals once again. Although the Lakers lost, Johnson was gracious in defeat. Always a class act, he entered the rival Bulls' locker room and congratulated the team on a job well done.

Three o'clock on November 7, 1991, arrives. Magic approaches the microphone. "Because I am infected with the HIV virus," he says, "I am retiring from basketball."

The announcement shook not just the sports world, but the whole world. Magic Johnson had retired from the game due to health reasons. The curtain officially came down on Showtime.

There would be no last second shots. No miracle comebacks. The time on Magic's career had run out. Teammates, friends, and fans alike shed tears. But Magic said, "I'm not down. Don't feel sorry for me, because if I died tomorrow, I've had the greatest life that anybody could ever imagine." As he spoke, he did what he had always done.

Johnson smiled.

Glossary

ALLEY-OOP. A long pass from the perimeter timed to meet a shooter leaping for the basket.

ASSIST. A pass that results directly in a basket.

BACK COURT. The area of the court that a team defends; also, another name for guards.

BALL HANDLER. The player who has control of the ball, often the point guard.

BANK SHOT. When the ball bounces off the glass or backboard and into the net.

DEFENSE. Guarding the team that has the ball. Also, the strategy used to keep the offense from scoring.

FAST BREAK. To run down court quickly, before the opposing team has an opportunity to switch to defense.

FIELD GOAL. A two-point basket.

FREE THROW. A penalty shot 15 feet from the basket, worth one point if successful.

FULL COURT PRESS. When each player on defense covers an opposing player closely down the length of the court, even before the opposite team has put the ball into play.

INTERCEPTION. Taking the ball away from the offensive team during a pass.

JUMP SHOT. A shot, usually one-handed, taken after a player has jumped straight up in the air.

OFFENSE. The team that has the ball, trying to score. Also, the strategy used to score and evade the defense.

OPEN MAN. A player without the ball who is in a good position to shoot.

PASS. To move the ball from one player to another, by either throwing or bouncing it.

POINT GUARD. The player who usually brings the ball upcourt, then controls the offense by starting a set play or by throwing a pass to an open man.

SET SHOT or TWO-HAND SET. A two-handed shot from the chest taken with both feet on the court, seldom used in today's game.

SHOOTING GUARD. A back court player whose primary role is to shoot rather than to set up plays.

STEAL. To take the ball away from an offensive player.

THREE-POINT SHOT. A shot taken from behind the three-point line.

Stats

All-Time NBA Assists Leaders†

	Years	Games	Assists	Avg.
Magic Johnson	12	874	9,921	11.4
Oscar Robertson	14	1,040	9,887	9.5
Isiah Thomas*	11	764	7,431	9.7
Lenny Wilkens	15	1,077	7,211	6.7
Maurice Cheeks*	13	1,010	7,100	7.0
Bob Cousy	14	924	6,955	7.5
Guy Rodgers	12	892	6,917	7.8
Nate Archibald	13	876	6,476	7.4
John Lucas	14	928	6,454	7.0
Reggie Theus*	13	1,026	6,453	6.3

†Through 1990-1991 season
*Still active

NBA Rookies Of The Year: Guards

Year	Player	Team	Pts.
1961	Oscar Robertson	Cincinnati	30.5
1967	Dave Bing	Detroit	20.0
1968	Earl Monroe	Baltimore	24.3
1974	Ernie DiGregorio	Buffalo	15.2
1978	Walter Davis	Phoenix	24.2
1979	Phil Ford	Kansas City	15.9
1981	Darrell Griffith	Utah	20.6
1985	Michael Jordan	Chicago	28.2
1988	Mark Jackson	New York	13.6
1989	Mitch Richmond	Golden State	22.0

Bibliography

Aaseng, Nate. *Basketball: You Are the Coach*. Minneapolis: Lerner Publications Company, 1983.

—. *Basketball's High Flyers*. Minneapolis: Lerner Publications Company, 1980.

Anderson, Dave. *The Story of Basketball*. New York: William Morrow and Company, Inc., 1988.

Editors of Sports Illustrated. *Sports Illustrated Basketball*. New York: J.B. Lippincott Company, 1971.

Finney, Shan. *Basketball*. New York: Franklin Watts, 1982.

Hirshberg, Al. *Basketball's Greatest Stars*. New York: G. P. Putnam's Sons, 1963.

Hollander, Zander, ed. *The Complete Handbook of Pro Basketball*. New York: Signet, 1991.

Liss, Howard. *Basketball Talk For Beginners*. New York: Julian Messner, 1970.

Meserole, Mike, ed. *The 1992 Information Please Sports Almanac*. Boston: Houghton Mifflin.

Olney, Ross. *Basketball*. Racine, Wisconsin: Western Publishing Company, Inc., 1975.

Ostler, Scott and Steve Springer. *Winnin' Times*. New York: Macmillan Publishing Company, 1988.

Rainbolt, Richard. *Basketball's Big Men*. Minneapolis: Lerner Publications Company, 1975.

Riley, Pat. *Showtime*. New York: Warner Books, Inc., 1988.

Ryan, Bob. *The Boston Celtics*. New York: Addison-Wesley Publishing Company, Inc., 1989.

Siegener, Ray, ed. *The Basketball Skill Book*. New York: Atheneum, 1974.

Sullivan, George. *Winning Basketball*. New York: David McKay Company, Inc., 1976.

Photo Credits

Allsport USA: 4, 8 (J. Daniel); 7, 10, 34 (Ken Levine); 15, 16, 18 (Tim DeFrisco); 19 (Jim Gund); 21, 38 (Damien Strohmeyer); 24, 28, 40 (Stephen Dunn); 26, 32 (Mike Powell)

Basketball Hall of Fame: 12, (Edward J. and Gina G. Hickox Library)

UPI/Bettman: 31

Wide World Photos: 23

Index